Crafting success: The Essential Guide to Starting a Small Business

Table of content

Introduction

Introduction

Starting a small business has become increasingly appealing in today's dynamic and ever-evolving business landscape. People are looking for opportunities to put their creative ideas into action, pursue their interests, and forge their own path to success as a result of the rise of entrepreneurship. However, launching and managing a small business can be a daunting endeavor that is fraught with numerous difficulties, ambiguities, and complexities.

Making Success Work: The Essential Guide to Starting a Small Business is a valuable and comprehensive guide that provides aspiring entrepreneurs with the knowledge, abilities, and tactics they need to navigate the complexities of building a successful business. Whether you fantasy about opening a shop store, sending off a tech startup, or offering particular types of assistance, this book fills in as your confided in buddy, giving pragmatic direction and master bits of knowledge to assist you with creating your own way to progress.

Crafting Success is a single, accessible volume that distills years of experience and knowledge written by industry experts and seasoned entrepreneurs. It covers every step in starting a small business, from thinking about it to doing it. This guide provides you with the necessary tools to turn your business idea into a thriving reality by examining key topics like business planning, market research, funding options, legal considerations, branding, marketing, and customer acquisition.

Crafting Success stands out thanks to its emphasis on practicality and adaptability to the real world. It goes past hypothetical ideas and gives significant exhortation, bit by bit directions, and contextual investigations that delineate prescribed procedures and feature normal entanglements to keep away from. This guide offers a path to success that can be tailored to your particular circumstances and goals, whether you are an experienced entrepreneur looking to improve your strategies or a first-time business owner looking to learn the basics.

Additionally, Crafting Success acknowledges the significance of human capital in entrepreneurship. It delved into topics like leadership, resilience, adaptability, and efficient decision-making to investigate the mindset and characteristics required to thrive as a small business owner. By tending to the individual and close to home parts of business, this book assists you with developing the fundamental attributes and perspectives to defeat difficulties and support long haul achievement.

In our current reality where private ventures assume an imperative part in driving development, setting out business open doors, and adding to monetary development, Making Achievement fills in as a fundamental ally for the people who hope against hope enormous and set out on the pioneering venture. This guide has the inspiration, inspiration, and practical advice you need to navigate the complexities of starting and running a small business, whether you are just starting out or have already started planning. Prepare to craft your own success story and turn your passion into money!

Chapter 1

Think and act like an Entrepreneur

Being an entrepreneur requires more than just having an idea for a business or starting one. It includes a way of thinking, a set of characteristics, and a strategy for dealing with challenges and opportunities. Thinking like an entrepreneur is fundamentally about being innovative, resourceful, and proactive in all spheres of life, not just business.

Adopting a mindset that seeks to solve problems is one of the most important aspects of entrepreneurial thinking. Entrepreneurs are skilled at recognizing market issues, gaps, or unmet needs and devising inventive solutions to address them. They are willing to take calculated risks in order to pursue novel projects and ideas because they see challenges as opportunities.

A strong sense of self-belief and confidence are also essential components of entrepreneurial thinking. Most of the time, entrepreneurs are trailblazers who go where no one else has gone before and take unconventional routes. They have the conviction to seek after their dreams, in any event, when confronted with doubt or misfortunes. They are able to persevere in the face of adversity, gain knowledge from their mistakes, and continuously modify and refine their strategies thanks to this mindset.

A strong sense of initiative and a preference for action are additional characteristics of an entrepreneurial mindset. Entrepreneurs are proactive and initiate the implementation of their concepts. They don't sit around waiting for opportunities to come their way; all things being equal, they effectively search them out and will invest the important energy and commitment to get things going.

In addition, adopting a growth mindset is necessary in order to think like an entrepreneur. Entrepreneurs constantly strive to acquire new skills, increase their knowledge, and stay ahead of the competition. They are open to constructive criticism and feedback and see challenges as learning opportunities. To remain relevant in a business environment that is rapidly changing, they are adaptable and willing to change their strategies as needed.

Entrepreneurial thinking also relies heavily on networking and collaboration. Entrepreneurs know how important it is to cultivate relationships, look for mentors, and have a supportive network around them. They foster partnerships and collaborations that amplify their impact and assist them in achieving their objectives by leveraging the expertise and strengths of others.

In conclusion, adopting an entrepreneurial mindset emphasizes problem-solving, self-assurance, initiative, ongoing education, adaptability, and teamwork. Regardless of the context, it is a way to approach challenges and opportunities with an entrepreneurial spirit. People can realize their creative potential, seize opportunities, and have a lasting impact in their personal and professional lives by developing this mindset.

What Fears Do You Have?

When considering new ventures or taking risks, fear is a normal and common emotion. Aspiring entrepreneurs may experience a number of anxieties regarding entrepreneurship. The fear of failing, the fear of financial instability, the fear of being judged or criticized, and the fear of leaving one's comfort zone are all common anxieties.

It's vital to recognize and figure out these apprehensions. Be that as it may, it's similarly significant not to allow dread to keep you away from chasing after your fantasies. Perceive that dread is a typical piece of the enterprising excursion and that numerous effective business people have encountered comparable feelings of trepidation. You can overcome challenges and achieve your objectives if you accept fear as a motivator and make use of it to drive your determination and drive.

What if I fail?

For a lot of people who want to start their own business, the fear of failing is a big concern. The possibility of financial planning time, exertion, and assets into an endeavor, just to have it not succeed, can plague. However, it is essential to reframe failure as an opportunity for growth rather than a setback that lasts forever.

In any entrepreneurial journey, failure is a necessary component. It gives important examples, experiences, and amazing open doors for development. Many successful business owners have made mistakes along the way, and it is often through these mistakes that they have learned the skills and perseverance they need to stay in business for the long haul.

Rather than zeroing in on the apprehension about disappointment, shift your outlook to embrace a development situated viewpoint. Consider failure to be a stepping stone toward success. Adapt your strategies, learn from your mistakes, and persevere in the face of difficulties. You can turn setbacks into stepping stones toward achieving your entrepreneurial goals with a resilient mindset and a willingness to learn from failures.

Do I Really want a Strategy?

A common query among aspiring entrepreneurs is whether a business plan is required. A well-thought-out business plan can significantly increase the likelihood of success, despite the fact that there is no definitive answer.

Your entrepreneurial journey can be guided by a business plan. It frames your vision, mission, target market, cutthroat scene, showcasing systems, monetary projections, and that's only the tip of the iceberg. It gives you a structured framework that will help you make decisions, effectively allocate resources, and remain focused on your goals.

A marketable strategy likewise fills in as a significant device while looking for subsidizing from financial backers or monetary foundations. It demonstrates your market comprehension, business model, and capacity for revenue and profitability.

A business plan can still be very helpful, even if you don't plan to look for outside funding. It aids in the clarification of your business concept, the identification of potential obstacles and opportunities, and the formulation of a strategic strategy for achieving your goals.

A business plan is not a guarantee of success, but it does give you a solid foundation and a clear path to follow as you start your own business. It increases your chances of starting a profitable and long-lasting business by keeping you organized, focused, and accountable to your objectives. Getting There:

Arriving at progress is a multi-layered and individual excursion. It entails establishing objectives, developing a distinct vision, and taking deliberate actions to realize that vision. Each person's definition of success is based on their own values and goals. Perseverance, resilience, continuous learning, and maintaining a growth mindset are, however, some common principles that can help individuals achieve success. By keeping on track, adjusting to difficulties, and remaining consistent with your interests and values, you can explore the promising and less promising times of the excursion and make your adaptation of progress.

Mindfulness:

The cultivation of a state of present-moment awareness without judgment or attachment is the practice of mindfulness. Being fully present and paying conscious attention to our thoughts, feelings, and experiences is the goal. Mindfulness has the potential to significantly improve productivity, decision-making, and overall well-being when it comes to achieving success. People can improve their focus and concentration, manage stress more effectively, and make conscious choices that are in line with their values and goals by practicing mindfulness. It fosters a sense of fulfillment and contentment by allowing people to fully engage with their work and personal lives.

Life balance at work:

The ability to strike a balance between personal well-being and professional obligations is known as work-life balance. It is about successfully overseeing investment to focus on both work and individual life, guaranteeing that neither one of the perspectives overwhelms to the detriment of the other. Happiness, health, and long-term success all depend on having a work-life balance. It involves establishing healthy routines and boundaries, scheduling time for hobbies, self-care, and activities that rejuvenate and nourish personal relationships. People can increase their productivity, prevent burnout, and lead lives that are more satisfying and balanced by establishing a healthy work-life balance.

Carrying on with a Self-Completed Life:

Carrying on with a self-realized life implies living up to one's true capacity and turning into one's best self. It involves aligning one's actions and choices with one's personal values, interests, and strengths. Self-actualization is a never-ending journey of self-discovery, personal development, and fulfillment. It necessitates reflection, self-awareness, and a dedication to one's own growth. By chasing after significant objectives, participating in exercises that give pleasure and satisfaction, supporting valid connections, and living in arrangement with one's qualities, people can encounter a profound feeling of direction and carry on with a self-realized life. Finding contentment, personal contentment, and a sense of wholeness in all aspects of life are the goals.

In conclusion, setting goals, acting with purpose, and remaining true to one's passions and values are all necessary for success. Productivity, well-being, and decision-making all benefit from mindfulness. A healthy work-life balance is essential for happiness as a whole and prevents burnout. To achieve self-actualization, one must align one's values, interests, and actions in order to realize one's potential and find contentment. You can make a journey that is both meaningful and successful if you apply these principles to your life.

Chapter 2

How to get started

Starting your own business can be a fun and lucrative endeavor. Take into consideration the following steps to begin your journey toward entrepreneurship:

- Identify Your Expertise and Passion:
Begin by determining your areas of expertise and passion. What are you good at? What abilities and information do you have that can be transformed into a business thought? Find opportunities that complement your talents and interests.

- Investigate the market:
Conduct in-depth market research after you have an idea for a business to determine the demand, the competition, and whether or not your venture could be profitable. Know your target market's requirements and the unique ways in which your product or service can meet those requirements.

- Create a Business Strategy:
Your vision, mission, target market, marketing strategies, financial projections, and operational details should all be included in a comprehensive business plan. A well-organized business plan will help you get funding if you need it and serve as a road map for your company.

- Obtainable Financing:
Find out how much money you need to start and run your business. Investigate different funding choices like individual investment funds, advances, awards, or associations. Make a spending plan and monetary projections to guarantee you have adequate financing to take care of your startup expenses and beginning functional costs.

- Complete Legal Requirements and Register Your Business:
Register your company with the appropriate government agencies and acquire any required permits or licenses. To protect your business's

interests and ensure compliance with regulations, consult legal and accounting professionals.

- Organize Your Team:

Survey your staffing needs and begin constructing your group. You should surround yourself with talented people who share your vision and can help your business grow and succeed. Delegate liabilities and establish a positive workplace that encourages joint effort and development.

- Create a Marketing and Branding Plan:

Create a strong brand identity and a marketing plan to promote your products or services effectively. Use different promoting channels, like virtual entertainment, computerized publicizing, content showcasing, and organizing, to reach and connect with your interest group.

- Start and Repeat:

 Launch your business and begin providing services to your customers after laying the groundwork. Be open to making adjustments and enhancements as necessary and keep an eye on feedback as well as performance. Persistently evaluate market patterns, client inclinations, and industry improvements to remain cutthroat and important.

Planning Strategically:

The process of establishing objectives, determining tactics, and making decisions for long-term success is known as strategic planning. It provides a framework for aligning the actions and resources of the organization with the business's overall vision and goals. The following are important strategic planning considerations:

- Vision and Mission:

 Characterize a convincing vision that mirrors your ideal future state and a mission that frames the reason and upsides of your business.

- Setting goals:

Supporting your vision, set specific, measurable, attainable, relevant, and time-bound (SMART) goals. Create goals for the short term as well as the long term that are in line with your overall strategic direction.

- Creation of a Strategy:

Make plans to reach your objectives. Consider factors, for example, market situating, separation, target market division, item/administration improvement, evaluating, dispersion, and showcasing.

- Resource distribution:

Evaluate the resources required to effectively implement your strategies. Decide the distribution of monetary, human, and mechanical assets to help your essential drives.

- Execution and Observing:

Foster an activity plan that frames the undertakings, obligations, courses of events, and measurements for checking progress. Consistently track key execution markers (KPIs) and change procedures on a case by case basis to keep focused.

- Continuous Assessment and Modification:

Make adjustments to your strategies based on the results of your regular evaluations of their efficacy.

Making Your product an Answer:

To make your item an answer, it's vital to comprehend your interest group and their trouble spots. Put yourself in their shoes, and consider the following: What difficulties or issues would they say they are confronting? What do they want and need? You can develop a product that directly addresses their specific problems or fulfills their desires by developing a deep understanding of your customers.

Center around the exceptional incentive of your item. Clearly explain how your product provides a significant advantage over other market alternatives or solves a specific problem. Draw attention to features and benefits that address the problems your target audience faces. You will be able to attract customers who are actively looking for a solution if you position your product as a solution.

Pricing Your product:

Deciding the right cost for your item requires cautious thought. Evaluating is a fragile harmony between taking care of your expenses, producing benefit, and offering a cutthroat value that clients will pay. There are a few things to think about:

- Cost Evaluation:

Ascertain every one of the expenses related with creating and conveying your item, including unrefined substances, producing, bundling, delivery, and above costs. Make sure you know exactly how your costs are structured.

- Analyses of the Competition:

Research the evaluating of comparable items on the lookout. Compare their characteristics, quality, and positioning to yours. You can use this analysis to see where your product stands in terms of price and value.

- Seen Worth:

Survey the apparent worth of your item according to your objective clients. Take into consideration the distinctive advantages, features, and any added value your product offers. In the event that clients see your item as predominant or more attractive, they might pay a premium.

- Estimating System:

Select a pricing strategy that is compatible with your company's objectives and target market. Cost-plus pricing, market-based pricing, value-based pricing, and penetration pricing are available options. Choose the strategy that best fits your product and market dynamics because each strategy has benefits and drawbacks.

Keep in mind that pricing is not a one-time choice. Assess your pricing strategy on a regular basis in light of your business goals, customer feedback, and the state of the market. Be open to adjusting prices as necessary to maintain competitiveness and maximize profitability.

Avoiding Being a Problem in Search of a Solution:

It is essential to begin with comprehensive market research in order to avoid becoming a solution in search of a problem. Prior to putting critical time and assets into fostering an item, approve its reasonability by evaluating the market interest.

Engage early with potential customers. To learn about their wants, needs, and preferences, conduct focus groups, interviews, or surveys. Utilize the feedback you receive to iterate on your product concept. You will have a better chance of developing a product that meets the specific requirements and desires of your target audience if you involve them in the process of development.

Moreover, watch out for market patterns and changes. Keep up with changes in the industry, how people behave, and new technologies. You can proactively identify new opportunities or alter your product strategy if necessary by remaining informed and adaptable.

In summary, you can increase your chances of developing a successful product that meets customer needs by concentrating on making your product a solution, setting a reasonable price for it, and carrying out comprehensive market research. Keep in mind to take in feedback on a regular basis, modify your strategy, and remain adaptable to changing market dynamics.

Chapter 3

Your Offer

Focusing on Clients:

Define your ideal customer profile before determining your target audience. Your product or service-related factors should form the basis of this profile. To help you narrow down your target audience, here are some additional things to think about:

Behavior: Take into account the habits and behaviors of your potential customers. Do they make more cautious purchases or are they early adopters? Do they prefer in-person experiences or online shopping? Your marketing strategies can be tailored in response to your understanding of their behavior.

Beliefs and Values: Consider the beliefs and values held by your target audience. Do they place a higher value on luxury, convenience, or sustainability? A strong emotional connection can be made if your brand's values are in line with those of your target audience.

Influencers: Determine the key opinion leaders or influencers in your target market. These people or gatherings can fundamentally affect forming buyer conduct and can be important partners in advancing your item or administration.

Understanding Your Clients:

Consider employing a variety of research strategies and instruments to learn more about your customers:
Surveys of Customers: To collect both quantitative and qualitative data from your target audience, design and distribute surveys. Pose inquiries about their inclinations, fulfillment levels, and ideas for development. This immediate input can uncover significant experiences into their requirements and assumptions.

Client Meetings: To learn more about customers' experiences, challenges, and motivations, conduct one-on-one interviews. This subjective methodology considers more inside and out investigation of their viewpoints and sentiments.

Virtual Entertainment Tuning in and Observing: Keep an eye on social media platforms to listen to conversations about your business, products, or rivals. Pay close attention to hashtags, mentions, and discussions in communities that are relevant. A wealth of information about customer sentiments, issues, and emerging trends can be gleaned from this real-time feedback.

Analytics for websites: You can get useful information about your website visitors by making use of website analytics tools like Google Analytics. Understand user preferences and behavior by analyzing metrics like page views, bounce rates, and time spent on the site.

Choosing a Market Segment:

By dividing your target audience into distinct groups or segments based on shared characteristics, you can segment your market. Common approaches to segmentation include:
Segmentation of Benefits: Customers should be divided into groups according to the particular advantages they seek from your product or service. For instance, a wellness application might have portions for weight reduction, muscle gain, or stress decrease.

Utilization Division: Segment customers based on how much or how frequently they use your product. This can assist you in adapting your product offerings and marketing messages to various usage patterns.

Segmentation by Occasion: Segment customers according to the occasions or particular circumstances in which they utilize your product. This permits you to tweak your informing to line up with their necessities during those particular minutes.

Geographic Division: Portion in view of geographic area, considering social contrasts, provincial inclinations, or neighborhood market elements. Businesses that have specific geographic targets will especially benefit from this.

You can create targeted marketing campaigns and personalized experiences that resonate with each segment of your market by effectively segmenting it. This permits you to expand the effect of your informing and better take special care of the novel requirements and inclinations of various client gatherings.

Keep in mind that customer preferences and market dynamics can change over time; consequently, you should regularly reevaluate and modify your strategies for targeting and segmentation. You will be able to adapt to and succeed in a dynamic market if you continue to learn about your customers and remain attentive to their changing requirements.

Competitors directly:
Businesses that offer similar or identical goods or services to yours and target the same customer segments are considered direct competitors. They compete directly for the same market share and operate in the same sector. Some important information about direct competitors:

Similarity in Product: In terms of features, benefits, and target market, your direct competitors' offerings are very similar to yours. They may have unique selling propositions or slight variations, but they generally satisfy the same customer requirements.

Overlap of Markets: Direct contenders focus on a similar client sections and vie for their consideration and buying choices. Because they frequently operate in the same market or geographic region, it is essential to differentiate your products and services from those of your rivals.

Positioning and Pricing: Your pricing strategies and market positioning are more likely to be influenced by direct competitors. To ensure that you remain competitive and compelling to your target customers, it is essential to monitor and analyze their pricing models, promotional activities, and brand positioning.

Analyses of the Competition: It is essential to carry out a comprehensive competitive analysis of your direct competitors. This entails investigating their products, marketing strategies, customer service, strengths, weaknesses, market share, and other aspects. This analysis helps you find opportunities, differentiate your brand, and improve your product and marketing plans.

Circuitous Contenders:

Businesses that offer products or services that are not identical to yours but serve a similar need or indirectly target the same customer base are considered indirect competitors. They may not be directly competing with you, but they can still affect your market share and the choices that customers make. Here are a few significant focuses about circuitous contenders:

Differentiation of a Product: Roundabout contenders offer items or administrations that are not the same as yours yet address comparable client needs or wants. Customers may take into consideration the alternatives they offer when making their purchasing decisions.

Portion of the overall industry Effect: Customers' preferences can be influenced and potential customers may be diverted away from your offerings by indirect competitors. Understanding their value proposition and determining the features that draw customers to their products are crucial. With this knowledge, you can effectively differentiate your offerings and refine your marketing messages.

Identifying Competitors Who Are Not Direct: Distinguishing circuitous contenders can be more difficult than direct contenders since they may not work in a similar industry or be effectively conspicuous. Direct statistical surveying and dissect client conduct to reveal elective arrangements or items that clients should think about instead of yours.

Possibilities for Collaboration: At times, circuitous contenders can likewise introduce joint effort open doors. You might look into partnerships or strategic alliances to tap into shared customer bases and create mutual benefits if their offerings complement yours or cater to a different stage of the customer journey.

Understanding both immediate and roundabout contenders is pivotal for creating successful promoting methodologies and situating your items or administrations on the lookout. By intently checking and examining your opposition, you can distinguish areas of separation, exploit one of a kind offering focuses, and persistently work on your contributions to remain serious in the commercial center.

Positioning strategically

The deliberate process of creating a unique and favorable perception of your brand or product in the minds of your target customers in comparison to your competitors is referred to as strategic positioning. It entails making deliberate decisions regarding how to position and differentiate your offerings in order to gain a competitive advantage. Here are the vital parts and contemplations for key situating:

Definition of the Target Market: It is essential to clearly define your target market prior to establishing your strategic position. Recognize the particular client fragments you intend to serve. Grasp their requirements, inclinations, and problem areas to successfully tailor your situating system.

Unique Proposition of Value (UVP): The central component of your strategic positioning is your distinctive value proposition. It responds to the query: What separates your item or brand from contenders?" Recognize and express the key advantages, elements, or traits that make your contributions interesting and important to clients.

Analyses of the Competition: Analyze your rivals thoroughly to learn about their positioning strategies and discover opportunities or gaps. Analyze their pricing, messaging, and customer perceptions as well as their strengths and weaknesses. This analysis helps you find areas in which your brand can stand out and be positioned in a unique way.

Method of Differentiation: A crucial aspect of strategic positioning is differentiation. Find out what sets your products apart from the competition. Think about features, quality, price, customer service, innovation, convenience, and sustainability of the product. To create a positioning statement that is both clear and persuasive, emphasize and convey these distinguishing characteristics.

Needs of the Customers: Your target customers' specific wants, needs, and issues should inform your strategic positioning. To position your brand or product as the ideal answer to their problems or desires, you need to comprehend their motivations, preferences, and challenges. Make sure your branding and messaging are in line with their goals and values.

Communication and messaging for the brand: Create a strong and consistent strategy for communicating your brand's positioning. Create compelling messages that resonate with your target audience and clearly convey your unique value proposition. A memorable and distinctive brand identity can be created by employing consistent language, images, and narrative.

Experience with Customers: Marketing messages are just one aspect of strategic positioning. It stretches out to the whole client experience. From pre-purchase interactions to post-purchase support, make sure that every touchpoint reflects your desired brand perception. Deliver on the promises and expectations that you set with your positioning strategy consistently.

Capacity to Adapt Over Time: Key situating isn't static; It needs to be checked and adjusted on a regular basis. Screen changes on the lookout, client inclinations, and cutthroat scene. Persistently assess and refine your situating procedure to remain applicable, profit by arising patterns, and keep up with your strategic advantage.

Keep in mind that a clear differentiation strategy, a thorough analysis of your competitors, and a thorough comprehension of your target market are all necessary for successful strategic positioning. You can gain a long-term competitive advantage in the market by creating a distinctive and favorable brand perception, which will also help you acquire and keep customers, cultivate brand loyalty, and attract new ones.

Chapter 4

Your plan of action

Promotion:
All of your efforts to communicate and market your product or service to your intended audience are included in promotion. Some important aspects of promotion include:

Advertising: To raise awareness and get your message out to a large number of people, make use of a variety of platforms, including print media, radio, television, online platforms, and social media. Create compelling advertising campaigns that emphasize your product or service's distinctive features and benefits.

PR (public relations): To increase your brand's visibility and enhance its reputation, cultivate positive relationships with stakeholders like the media, influencers, and other stakeholders. To project a positive image of your brand, take part in activities like press releases, events, sponsorships, and community involvement.

Promotion of Sales: Incentives, discounts, or special deals that only last a short time are all good ways to get customers to buy right away or make them feel like they have to. Buy one, get one free offers, coupon codes, loyalty programs, and free gifts with a purchase are all examples.

Individual Selling: Use account managers, customer service representatives, or sales representatives to interact directly with customers and provide them with individualized information and support to help them make a purchase. Fabricate connections, address client various forms of feedback, and feature the worth of your item or administration.

Content Promoting: Make significant and applicable substance, for example, blog entries, recordings, infographics, or webcasts, to connect with and teach your ideal interest group. Foster a substance technique that lines up with your clients' advantages and trouble spots, situating your image as a legitimate and dependable asset.

Place:

The distribution channels and strategies you employ to make your product or service accessible to customers are referred to as "place." Here are a few contemplations for successful spot methodologies: Choice of Channel: Decide the most appropriate dispersion channels for your item. Consider alternatives like wholesalers, distributors, retail stores, e-commerce platforms, and direct sales. Reach, cost-effectiveness, and compatibility with the preferences of your target audience are all important considerations.

Retail Presence: In the event that you settle on actual retail stores, cautiously pick store areas in view of variables, for example, pedestrian activity, socioeconomics, and contenders' presence. Make certain that your products are attractively displayed and that the shopping experience is consistent with your brand's image.

E-commerce: Make use of online platforms to sell your goods worldwide or reach more people. Create a secure and user-friendly e-commerce website, optimize it for search engines, and think about forming partnerships with online marketplaces to broaden your customer base.

Management of the Supply Chain: Manage the flow of products from production or manufacturing to the customer. To meet customer expectations and minimize delays, establish dependable logistics, inventory management processes, and fulfillment strategies.

Your Sales Strategy:

The strategies, goals, and actions you will take to reach your sales goals are laid out in a sales plan. Here are a critical components to consider while making your deals plan:
Goals for Sales: Make sales goals that are specific, measurable, and attainable that are in line with your company's goals. Separate them into more modest achievements and track progress consistently. Make sure your objectives are difficult but doable.

Target Market Division: Prioritize the customer segments you will concentrate on by identifying them. To effectively tailor your sales strategies and messages, you need to comprehend their requirements, preferences, and pain points. This assists you with allotting assets effectively and concentrate endeavors where they will yield the best yield.

Sales Methods: Identify the specific sales strategies you will use to engage and reach your target audience. This could be done through social selling, networking, cold calling, online demonstrations, email campaigns, or referrals. Set up sales processes and workflows as well as define the roles and responsibilities of your sales team.

Enablement and Training for Sales: In order to improve your sales team's product knowledge, sales techniques, and customer engagement skills, provide ongoing training and support.

Growth

Anticipating development and change is a basic part of developing your endeavor and guaranteeing long haul achievement. It requires a comprehensive and in-depth strategy to strategically adapt your business to scale and change, identify opportunities, and anticipate future requirements. Planning for expansion and expanding your business should take these important factors into account:

Evaluating Current Execution:

Analyze your company's current performance thoroughly. Analyze important metrics like profitability, sales, revenue, and customer acquisition. Identify your strengths and areas for development. For insights into your position in the market and potential growth areas, examine market trends, the competitive landscape, and customer feedback.

Setting goals for growth:

Establish specific, measurable, attainable, relevant, and time-bound (SMART) goals to achieve your growth goals. Your overall business vision should be reflected in these objectives, which should give you a clear direction for your growth efforts.

Consider both present moment and long haul objectives to guarantee a fair way to deal with development.

Statistical surveying and Investigation:

To comprehend the requirements of your target audience and customers, conduct extensive market research. Discover new trends, consumer preferences, and innovation opportunities.
Examine the landscape of your rivals to find areas where you can stand out and fill in the gaps. To strategically position your business, comprehend the strengths and weaknesses of your competitors.

Establishing a Growth Plan:

Create a growth strategy that outlines the key initiatives and actions required to achieve your goals based on your goals and market research. Find the most effective strategies for expanding your business, such as entering new geographical markets, focusing on new customer segments, creating new goods or services, or broadening your product or service range.
Think about making acquisitions, partnerships, or collaborations that can help you grow faster or give you access to new technologies or markets.
Planning for Resources:

Evaluate the resources required to implement your growth strategies. Human capital, technology, and infrastructure are all included in this. Explore various financing options, such as loans, investment partnerships, and government grants, to determine the funding requirements for your growth initiatives.
Create a comprehensive budget and financial projections that are in line with your growth goals and demonstrate your plans' viability.

Efficiency in the Workplace:

Smooth out and improve your functional cycles to help development. Management of the supply chain, production procedures, inventory management, and customer service are all areas where efficiency can be increased.

Put money into systems and technologies that can automate and streamline operations, boost productivity, and make the customer experience better.

Persistently screen and measure functional execution to distinguish bottlenecks or regions for development.

Creating a Stable Team:

Make an investment in the formation of a team with the skills and drive to support your plans for growth. Hire talented people who are a good fit for your company's culture and have the knowledge you need to grow. Create a positive work environment that encourages creativity, teamwork, and ongoing education. In order to empower your employees and boost their capabilities, provide training and development opportunities.

Energize cross-useful coordinated effort and make channels for open correspondence to guarantee arrangement and cooperative energy inside your group.

Flexibility and creativity:

To stay ahead of the competition and adapt to changing market demands, cultivate a culture of innovation.

Urge your group to think imaginatively, investigate groundbreaking thoughts, and trial with inventive ways to deal with items, administrations, or plans of action.

To proactively identify opportunities for innovation and adapt your strategies accordingly, keep up with industry trends, technological advancements, and customer preferences.

Adjustment and evaluation on a regular basis:

Make any necessary adjustments to your strategies and plans after conducting regular assessments of your progress toward your growth objectives.

In order to evaluate the efficacy of your growth initiatives, keep an eye on key performance indicators (KPIs), track customer feedback, and carry out periodic reviews.

Be flexible and willing to change.

How much money you need.

While beginning or growing a business, one of the key inquiries that emerges is, "How much cash do I really need, and where does the cash come from?" Let's casually examine these aspects, which include equity funding.

What amount do I really require?

The objectives of your business, the costs of running it, and your plans for expansion all need to be carefully considered before you can figure out how much money you need.

To get started, develop a comprehensive budget that outlines the anticipated costs you anticipate for things like staffing, rent, utilities, equipment, product development, and marketing.

Take into account both the one-time startup costs and the ongoing operational costs.

Make sure you have money set aside for unforeseen difficulties by taking into account any costs that are unanticipated or unplanned.

While your company is still in its infancy and may not generate a significant amount of revenue, you should take into account your personal financial requirements, including living costs.

In order to ensure that you have sufficient capital to support and expand your business, it is always prudent to overestimate your financial requirements.

Where is the money obtained?

Your company has access to a number of potential funding options. The most typical of these are:

Individual Reserve funds:

To start their businesses, many people borrow money from their own savings. Despite the potential for personal financial risks, this allows for complete financial control.

Family and Friends: You can move toward dear companions or relatives who trust in your business thought and will put away or loan you cash.

Having clear agreements and approaching these arrangements professionally is essential.

Lender Loans:
One common choice for financing is to take out loans from banks. If you need a loan, you can approach banks and other financial institutions based on your creditworthiness, business plan, and collateral.

Loans from the Small Business Administration (SBA):
In certain nations, government-upheld advance projects, like those presented by the SBA, give funding choices explicitly intended to private companies. A lot of the time, these loans come with favorable terms and lower interest rates.

Contests and Grants:
Take part in entrepreneurial competitions that provide winners with financial incentives such as investments or grants for businesses. The preparation of grant applications or competition pitches and extensive research are required for these options.

Crowdfunding:
Use online stages where people can contribute modest quantities of cash to help your business thought. You can showcase your product or service and get backers on crowdfunding platforms.

Private supporters:
Private supporters are people or gatherings who put their own cash in new companies in return for value or possession stakes. In addition to funding, they frequently provide expertise and mentorship.

Capital for ventures:
In exchange for equity, venture capital firms make larger investments in high-potential startups. Businesses with significant growth potential and a scalable business model are typically their primary focus.

Strategic alliances:

Look into the possibility of forming strategic alliances with investors or businesses that can support you financially while also giving you access to more resources or markets.

Equity Capital:

Equity funding is the process of selling investors ownership stakes or shares in your company to raise money.
When looking for significant capital for businesses with high growth, this type of funding is frequently used.
With equity financing, investors can become shareholders in your business and potentially contribute their knowledge, connections, and direction.
You need to create a compelling business plan, highlight the market potential of your product or service, and highlight the capabilities of your team if you want equity funding.
Equity funding typically comes from venture capitalists, angel investors, and certain crowdfunding platforms.
Consider carefully the terms and conditions of any investment offers because equity funding entails sharing ownership and control of your business.
Keep in mind that identifying your financial requirements and obtaining funding are ongoing processes. It is essential to regularly reevaluate your financial situation, make any necessary adjustments to your budget, and investigate various funding options.

Chapter 5

Composing your strategy

Entrepreneurs frequently ask themselves whether or not a business plan is necessary. While it might appear to be an overwhelming undertaking, having a thoroughly examined strategy can give various advantages and increment your odds of coming out on top. When deciding whether to create a business plan, consider the following:

Lucidity of Vision:

Your venture's vision can be better articulated and clarified with the help of a business plan. It forces you to give your business idea a lot of thought, set goals, and write down the steps you need to take to get there.
By reporting your vision, you make a guide that fills in as an aide for you and likely partners.

Vital Bearing:

A strategy gives an essential system to your business. It helps you prioritize important tasks, effectively allocate resources, and make well-informed decisions.
It permits you to expect difficulties, distinguish open doors, and foster techniques to relieve gambles and profit by market patterns.

Tool for communication:

A well-written business plan is a tool for sharing your ideas with potential partners, investors, lenders, or team members. It demonstrates your ability to carry out your plans, knowledge of the market, and landscape of competition.
It helps you make a convincing case for why your business is worth investing in and could succeed.

Planning your finances:

The financial section of a business plan, which includes projected revenues, expenses, and profitability, is an essential component. This enables you to plan for potential funding requirements and assess the financial viability of your business concept.

It enables you to make informed financial decisions by assisting you in comprehending your break-even point, cash flow requirements, and return on investment.

Here are a few things you should know about writing a business plan:

Analyses of the Market and Research:

Prior to composing your field-tested strategy, direct intensive exploration on your objective market, industry patterns, client needs, and serious scene. Your plan's relevance and viability are assured by this information, which serves as its foundation.

Get to Know Your Customers:

Learn a great deal about the people you want to sell to. Learn about their needs, preferences, and purchasing habits. You can effectively tailor your products, services, and marketing strategies to meet their needs with this information.

Analyses of the Competition:

Learn about your rivals' strengths, weaknesses, and market positioning by analyzing them. You can develop strategies to gain a competitive advantage and differentiate your offerings with the assistance of this analysis.

Define Your Standout Advantage:

Obviously eloquent your novel incentive, which separates your business from rivals. Determine the most important features, advantages, and benefits that draw customers to your products or services.

Realistic Estimates of the Economy:

Based on extensive research into the market and industry standards, make financial projections that are based on reality. Guarantee your income conjectures, cost gauges, and net revenues are grounded actually. Plan for Operations and Implementation:

Outline your company's operational aspects, such as its organizational structure, distribution channels, marketing and sales strategies, and production procedures. Give specifics about the actions you'll take to successfully implement your business plan.
Keep in mind that a business plan is an ever-evolving document that can change over time. Make changes to your plan on a regular basis to keep up with market shifts, industry trends, and your company's progress.

Leader Rundown:

The executive summary is a brief overview of your project that serves as an introduction to your business plan.
Start with a compelling opening statement that draws the reader in and emphasizes your company's unique value to the market.
Give a short depiction of your business idea, making sense of what issue you are tackling and how your item or administration resolves that issue.
Include a summary of your target market that highlights its size, growth potential, and any significant trends or insights that make it appealing.
Highlight your advantage over your rivals by emphasizing what sets your company apart from its rivals and the reasons why customers would choose your product or service.
Frame your monetary projections, including key income streams, productivity, and projected development. A brief overview of your company's financial potential ought to be provided in this section.

Pitch of the Lift:

A brief presentation is a succinct and convincing outline of your business that can be conveyed in a short measure of time, normally 30-60 seconds.
To get the listener's attention and pique their interest, begin with a catchy hook or question.

Make your product or service's problem or need relatable and compelling by clearly communicating it.

Point out how your unique solution solves the problem better or more efficiently than other options.

Focus on the outcomes your product can help customers achieve by highlighting the advantages and value it offers.

Engage the listener and leave a lasting impression by employing persuasive language and storytelling strategies.

Organization Outline:

The history, mission, vision, values, and legal structure of your company are all covered in detail in the company overview.

Describe the inspiration for your business and how it has developed over time in your venture's story.

Clearly define your company's purpose and long-term objectives by defining your mission and vision.

Describe the guiding principles and core values that guide your decision-making and shape your company's culture.

Showcase the relevant experience and skills of key team members, highlighting their qualifications and expertise.

Talk about any strategic alliances, collaborations, or partnerships that help your company grow and succeed.

Mention any intellectual property, patents, or proprietary technology that sets you apart from competitors and gives you an advantage.

Description of the item:

Give a far reaching and nitty gritty portrayal of your item or administration, making sense of its key highlights, functionalities, and advantages.

Clearly explain how your product addresses a specific market need or solves a specific issue.

Feature the interesting selling focuses and benefits that put your item aside from contenders.

Make use of descriptive language to convey the qualities, performance, and user experience of your product in vivid detail.

Show, if necessary, how your product works with other products or services or integrates with existing systems.

Include any relevant endorsements, awards, or certifications that attest to your product's credibility and quality.

Keep in mind that the purpose of your introduction is to captivate your audience, make it clear how valuable your project is, and pique their interest in further investigation. Use language that connects with your target audience, provide compelling evidence of your company's viability and uniqueness, and leave a lasting impression that piques interest and encourages engagement.

Conclusion

All through the book, we have investigated different parts of building and growing a fruitful business, giving experiences, tips, and methodologies to explore the difficult yet compensating excursion of business venture.

This book has covered essential topics that lay the groundwork for a successful venture, including understanding the entrepreneurial mindset, developing a strategic plan, pricing your product, and identifying your target market. We've discussed the four Ps of marketing, promotion, location, sales planning, and the significance of effective marketing.

We have also looked at how important it is to plan your finances, manage your resources, and make a solid management and staffing plan to help your business grow. We have underscored the requirement for a very much created strategy, illustrating the critical parts and contemplations prior to leaving on the creative cycle.

In addition, we have talked about how important it is to embrace change, encourage innovation, and plan for growth. To ensure long-term success, we have stressed the importance of adaptability, ongoing education, and a healthy work-life balance.

We have promoted mindfulness, self-awareness, and the pursuit of self-actualization throughout this journey. By adjusting your interests and values to your business, you can make an endeavor that brings monetary accomplishment as well as satisfaction and a feeling of direction.

Using Crafting Success as a guide, you'll learn how to overcome obstacles, take advantage of opportunities, and succeed as an entrepreneur. It is a guide that encourages strategic thinking, customer-centeredness, and innovation. It stresses the significance of resilience, tenacity, and remaining true to your vision.

Keep in mind that starting your own business won't guarantee immediate success. It requires a willingness to learn from both successes and failures, dedication, and hard work. Be open to continuous improvement, remain committed to your goals, and surround yourself with a network of support.

This is more than just a book; it's a companion that gives you the knowledge, resources, and motivation you need to make your business goals a reality. Therefore, take advantage of the opportunity, rise to the challenges, and set out on a path that will lead you to your own success as an entrepreneur.

www.ingramcontent.com/pod-product-compliance
Lightning Source LLC
Chambersburg PA
CBHW070906220526
45466CB00005B/2142